THE LITTLE BOOK OF
WHISKY

Published in 2022 by OH!
An Imprint of Welbeck Non-Fiction Limited,
part of Welbeck Publishing Group.
Based in London and Sydney.
www.welbeckpublishing.com

ISBN 978-1-91161-097-7

Compiled and written by: Malcolm Croft
Editorial: Theresa Bebbington
Design: Tony Seddon
Project manager: Russell Porter
Production: Jess Brisley

A CIP catalogue record for this book is available from the British Library

Printed in China

10 9 8 7 6

Cover image: freepik.com

THE LITTLE BOOK OF
WHISKY

MATURED TO PERFECTION

CONTENTS

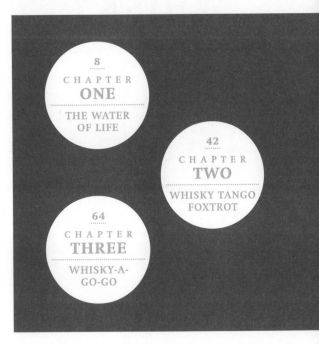

INTRODUCTION

No drink on earth can make a person go weak at the knees as much as whisky. There's something deeply intoxicating about this particular tipple, beyond the bonkers ABV, of course, as if it has a beguiling charm that makes those who gaze into its caramel cage fall under some enchanted spell. Put simply, it's hard not to get romantic about whisky. It's very existence is alchemy, *unbelievable chemistry* – the transformation of ordinary grains into something more than just an alcoholic beverage, a drink. It's an elixir. And it's a spirit, for sure, in the purest sense – it has a *life*, a *magic*, of its own and fills right up to the rim. And it is that life that we hope we have triple-distilled into this mini anthology, the words forever oak ageing between the pages. Sadly, we weren't allowed to alligator char the book, for obvious reasons.

For more than a millennia, humans have come together to savour the complex flavours of whisky; develop and pass on the processes of its creation; observe as to how it has evolved into a multi-billion pound industry and then into, today, unarguably, the most iconic – the *coolest* – spirit there has ever been.

Of course, whisky's history is as complex as its creation, with many things coming together: inventions and inventors and their magical machinery; heroes and villains; science and nature; and gadgets and gizmos – each one enhancing the experience with one singular purpose: *to taste the sublime*.

This tiny tome – think of it as your ideal drinking companion, your wing man, but one who won't get smashed after three Whiskey Sours – is a spirited whisky-soaked celebration of all things wet, wild and whisky-shaped. It's a compendium, a whisky-pedia, if you will, of all things great and small about this extra-special spirit distilled from, let's be honest, breakfast cereals.

This *Little Book of Whisky* is here to help you master the dark art of whisky appreciation, and all it asks in return is for you to sit down in your favourite chair, pour a *wee dram* of your whisky of choice and learn about the thing you love the most.

So, let's raise a glass to them good ol' boys (and girls) drinking whisky and rye (as Don McLean once famously sang in that song about pies) and celebrate in hope that today is the day you'll try a whisky that blows your socks off.

Like I said, whisky – it's hard not to get romantic about it.

Cheers!

CHAPTER
ONE

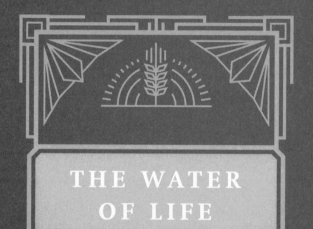

THE WATER
OF LIFE

Know Thy Whisky

Whisky comes in two forms:

Malt whisky is made primarily from malted barley.

Grain whisky is made from any type of cereal grain such as wheat, rye or corn.

Whisky then falls under these categories:

Single Malt

For Scotch to qualify as a single malt, the spirit must be made from a mash of 100 per cent malted barley and distilled at a single distillery by way of a pot still distillation process.

Single Grain
Single grain Scotch can incorporate any cereal grains (wheat, rye or corn; malted or unmalted) into the mash. The whisky must be distilled at a single distillery and it can be distilled continuously in continuous stills or column stills.

Blended Malt
A blend of single malt Scotch whiskies from two or more different distilleries.

Blended Grain
A blend of single grain Scotch whiskies from two or more different distilleries.

Blended Scotch
A blend of single malt and single grain Scotch whiskies.

Hop-Scotch No.1

There are 120 distilleries currently operating in Scotland. These distilleries operate within the five major whisky-producing regions:

1. Highlands
2. Lowlands
3. Campbeltown
4. Speyside
5. Islay

Each region famously brings its own distinct character and flavour to its whisky.

Hop-Scotch No.2

There are five regions of Scotland
that produce Scotch.

HIGHLANDS

Highland distilleries tend to be light,
fruity and spicy. The Highland region is
the biggest of all Scotland's five whisky
regions.

66

I'm on a whisky diet.
I've lost three days already.

99

Tommy Cooper

Whisky Business No.1

When legendary American crooner Frank Sinatra was buried in 1998 he took three items with him to the grave:

1. A pack of Camel cigarettes (his lucky smokes)
2. A roll of dimes (in case there was a payphone)
3. A bottle of Jack Daniels (his favourite whiskey)

The singer liked his two-finger pour of Jack on the rocks – three ice cubes, to be precise. First introduced to the drink in 1947, Sinatra would go on to drink little else. In 1955 Sinatra took to the stage and declared "Ladies and gentleman, this is Jack Daniel's and it's the nectar of the gods." By doing so, Sinatra took Jack Daniel's from being a small, regional brand to being a household name and made the Tennessee whiskey a pop-culture icon too.

Whisky Business No.2

Let's clear this up once and for all. "Whiskey", with an "e", is preferred by Irish and Americans drinkers. "Whisky", no "e", is preferred in Scotland, as well as Canada, Japan and the rest of the world. The reason is simple.

When Irish whisky producers began exporting their whisky to North America in the 1600s they wanted to differentiate their product from the, at the time, poor whisky made in Scotland by adding an extra "e" in the name.

True scotch is made only in Scotland. Bourbon, from Bourbon County, Kentucky, can be made outside of Kentucky, but must be made in the United States.

Whisky Chasers No.1

Whisky chasers always chasin' tail…

Old Fashioned

Go Get:
Two shots (50ml) of rye or bourbon whiskey
A tumbler
2 dashes Angostura bitters
1 sugar cube
Soda water
Orange Twist (garnish)

Make it Right:
- Place the sugar cube in a tumbler (also known as an old-fashioned glass).
- Splash in the Angostura bitters and a quick splash of soda water.
- Smash the sugar cube with a spoon, and ensure the sugar grains and bitters coat the glass. Add a large ice cube; pour in the shot of whiskey.
- Garnish with an orange twist.

Make Your Own Whisky: No.1

STEP ONE: Malting

The first of the five steps of whisky production is malting: turning starch in the barley into soluble sugars to make alcohol.

First, the barley must undergo germination; this is achieved by spreading the barley across a floor (or large drum) and soaking it for two or three days in warm water. When the barley starts to shoot, it needs to be stopped by heat and dried in a kiln. The dried barley is now called malt and it is ready to be ground down to a fine powder in a mill.

Make Your Own Whisky: No.2

STEP TWO: Mashing

The second of five steps of whisky production is known as mashing: grounding down the malt (dried barley), to a fine powder, called "grist". Warm water is then added; the water extracts the sugars from the grist. The water used here is very important – the purer, the better. It is why most distilleries anyway in the world are located next to a river or body of water (see page 140). Any minerals in the water (gained from flowing over granite, rock or soil such as peat) will be passed over into the water.

Adding water to the malt creates the "mash". The mash is put into a mash tun and stirred for many hours. Now, the sugars in the malt dissolve and are deposited at the bottom of the mash tun. What remains in the mash tun is a sugary liquid called "wort".

Make Your Own Whisky: No.3

STEP THREE: Fermentation

The third of five steps of whisky production is known as fermentation: the wort is cooled in large tanks called washback's. Yeast is now added to the wort and fermentation commences! The yeast turns sugars present in the wort into alcohol. The type of yeast added, as with the selection of particular types of barley and water, is all important. The strain of yeast chosen will have an effect on the whisky's final flavour.

Fermentation lasts 48 hours or so. The resulting liquid is called "wash". Typically it has a low alcohol strength, 5–10% ABV. At this stage the wash is, effectively, beer. The difference between beer and whisky is that you now distil the wash to make whisky, whereas you brew the wash to make beer.

Make Your Own Whisky: No.4

STEP FOUR: Distillation

The fourth of five steps in whisky production is known as distillation: separating the different components from the wash mixture by processes of boiling and condensation. Irish whiskey, typically, triple distils its wash, Scotch wash is distilled twice. Using a pair of bowl-shaped copper stills (the best material for extracting impurities from the wash) with long necks, the wash is fed into the first copper still and is heated. As it's heated, the liquid vaporises and rises up the neck of the still where it then condenses. Only the alcoholic liquid created during the middle (or "heart") of this distillation process goes on to become whisky – this liquid is skilfully removed by a stillman via a "spirit safe". The spirit, at this stage, has an alcoholic strength of 65–70% ABV.

Make Your Own Whisky: No.5

STEP FIVE: Maturation

The final step of five in whisky production is known as maturation: the distilled spirit is placed (predominately) into charred American white oak casks and stored. During this maturation stage, the flavours of the spirit fuse with natural compounds in the wood cask and this gives the whisky its unique character.

As wood is porous, the cask will absorb the air from its nearby environment, so the location of the casks is very important to the final flavour profiles. The longer the whisky is barrel/cask aged, the better!

"

A good gulp of hot whisky at bedtime – it's not very scientific, but it helps.

"

Alexander Fleming,*
the discoverer of penicillin, on how to kill a common cold

*Check out the Penicillin cocktail, created in Fleming's honour.

Whisky-a-lingo-go No.1

"Neat / Straight Up"
    In a glass, boom, done.

"On the Rocks"
    Whisky poured over ice in your glass. Only
    psychopaths do it the other way around.

"Up"
    Served in a chilled cocktail glass.

"With A Splash / Water Back"
    Whisky ordered "with a splash" means with a
    few drops of water added once whisky is in the
    glass. The dilution of the whisky helps soften
    the alcohol attack and allows your nose and
    tongue to smell and taste the flavours better, as
    proven by science. "Water back", means a glass
    of water on the side.

"With A Twist"
    Whisky, but poured over a large ball or cube of
    ice. Then, for that final flourish, garnished with
    a small twist of lemon, lime or orange peel. Any
    citrus fruit works wonders with whisky.

Whisky Around the World No.1

Whisky may be Ireland and Scotland's national drink, but it is in fact a spirit that belongs to the world. To celebrate, say "Cheers" in languages from all around the world:

Afrikaans: *Gesondheid!* (Ge-sund-hate)
Chinese (Mandarin): *Gān bēi!* (Gan-bay)
Czech: *Na zdravi!* (Naz-drah vi)
Dutch: *Proost!* (Prohst)
French: *Santé!* (Sahn-tay)
German: *Prost! / Zum wohl!* (Prohst / Tsum vohl)
Greek: *ΥΓΕΙΑ!* (Yamas)
Irish Gaelic: *Sláinte!* (Slawn-cha)
Italian: *Salute! / Cin cin!* (Saw-lutay / Chin chin)
Japanese: *Kanpai!* (Kan-pie)
Polish: *Na zdrowie!* (Naz-droh-vee-ay)
Spanish: *Salud!* (Sah-lud)

Whisky Business No.3

If this doesn't make you want to visit Scotland nothing will: the nation is currently home to more than *20 million casks* of maturing whisky.

That's four casks for every Scottish person. No wonder they want their independence.

Whisky History No.1

In Gaelic, whisky is translated to
"uisge beathe", which means – yes,
you've guessed it – "water of life".
Uisge came to be pronounced
(roughly) as *ouishky* and, well, the
rest is whisky history.

When the first word spread around
Europe, from the 11th century, no
one could pronounce *"uisge beathe"*,
so they shortened it to *uisge*, which
then evolved into our modern-day
spelling: whisky.

Whisky Business No.4

Every single second,
42 bottles of Scotch are shipped
from Scotland to more than
175 thirsty countries.

Whisky Business No.5

In order for Scottish whisky to be
called Scotch – a prestigious
distinction – the spirit must mature
in oak casks in Scotland for a
minimum of three years and one day.

Anything less, ain't Scotch.

Whisky at the Movies No.1
Name the film

"

Scotchy, scotch, scotch.
Here it goes down. Down
into my belly.

"

Anchorman

Whisky Wisdom No.1

Every May, when whisky enters its
maturation phase, approximately
2 per cent of the whisky in the cask is
lost via natural evaporation.

This lost whisky is called the Angels'
Share, or the Angels' Pinch.

66

When my ancestors were
determined of a set purpose to
be merie, they used a kind of
aqua vite, void of all spice, and
onelie consisting of such herbs
and roots as they grew in their
own gardens…

99

Hector Boece,
the first principal of Aberdeen University, and Scottish scolar,
writing in his 1527 text The History and Chronicles of
Scotland *about the medicinal value of whisky.*

Whisky Business No.6

"A dram of whisky" is a quaint Scottish colloquialism. For many, a dram refers to a single serving, or just a straight-talking glass of whisky.

It's origin dates back to when the spirit was considered medicinal and a dram was prescribed by doctors, but it was barely enough wetness to whet your appetite – less than a teaspoon. That's not enough whisky to cure anyone.

Whisky By the Numbers No.1

Scotch whisky must be bottled at a minimum strength of 40 per cent ABV (alcohol by aolume).

And, as proof must always equal double the ABV, Scotch whisky must be 80 per cent proof.

Whisky Business No.7

Which president of the United States was also the single largest producer of whisky in the country come the year 1799? Clue: he was also the first ever president.

George Washington.

66

You actually go down to Kentucky, Louisville, and they've got bourbons that make Old Grandad and Jack Daniels look like Schweppes bitter lemon…there's one called Rebel Yell and that's dynamite shit.

99

Keith Richards
When it comes to whisky, Keef knows his shit.

Spell A Rebel Yell

Billy Idol's hit 1983 "Rebel Yell" was inspired by the Kentucky bourbon brand. The song arrived in the singer's mind when Idol attended an awards event and saw the Rolling Stones Mick Jagger, Keith Richards and Ronnie Wood taking large swigs straight from a bottle of Rebel Yell.

Idol himself had never heard of the brand but liked the name enough to write the song.

66

You cannot drink gin and tonic in the middle of the night. You must have whisky to give you energy.

99

Margaret Thatcher

According to Thatcher's private diet notes, in 1979, the soon-to-be Prime Minister only allowed herself to imbibe whisky (and soda) "on days when meat is eaten. Otherwise, no alcohol." Meat days were Tuesdays, Wednesdays, Saturdays and Sundays.

Winston Churchill

For Winston Churchill, every day began
(at 8am) with a glass of Scotch whisky.
And a cigar. Churchill would sip his
Scotch and add water to it throughout the
day. The former Prime Minister's weapon
of choice was Johnnie Walker Red Label,
or Black Label.

Despite Churchill's daily devotion
to drinking there is no record of the
politician ever being drunk and disorderly
in public, which means his famous quote
– "I have taken more out of alcohol than
it has taken out of me" – is the truth.
Unique for a politician.

Cask a Question No.1

Do you know your barrel from your cask? You should: whisky casks are what give our precious water of life its 100+ flavour profile(s).

Casks come in all shapes and sizes, and remember: *90 per cent of Scotch whisky is stored in American-made bourbon barrels.*

The American Standard Barrel (ASB)

- Holds between 190–200 litres (300 bottles of 700ml whisky) and is used to store bourbon whiskey.
- By law, bourbon must be aged in new casks. After that, they are used, predominantly, to mature Scotch.
- ASB's are cheap compared with other types of cask.
- ASB's are made from new, pre-charred American white oak.
- ASB's are renowned for their trademark notes of coconut and vanilla.

Bourbon Whiskey

Bourbon is an American whiskey primarily made from 51 per cent corn mash and must be stored in charred oak casks – for no minimum amount of time, but usually more than two years. Anything less than four years, and the producer must state age.

Bourbon is a sweet tasting whiskey when compared to Scotch's smokiness. It does not need to be made in Bourbon, Kentucky, to be called Bourbon; it can be made anywhere within the borders of the United States.

Bourbon is the national spirit of that country – enjoyed there more than anyone else on earth – due, in part, to the fact that the rum, previously the nation's no.1 tipple, and imported from the Caribbean, was highly taxed. Home-grown grain, such as corn was not.

Tasting Table: *Knob Creek, Wild Turkey, Elijah Craig, Old Forester, Maker's Mark, Woodford Reserve*

CHAPTER
TWO

WHISKY TANGO
FOXTROT

Whisky Chasers No.2

Whisky chasers always chasin' tail…

Manhattan

Go Get:
Two shots (50ml) of rye whiskey
Half shot of Italian vermouth
Two splashes Angostura bitters
Ice, cracked
Lemon twist or cocktail cherry (garnish)

Make it Right:
- Mix the rye, vermouth and bitters together in your tumbler with the cracked ice.
- Strain the mixture into a chilled cocktail/ martini glass.
- Garnish with a twist and/or a cocktail cherry.

Know Your Char

Charring, and toasting, of whisky casks are a very important part of whisky production. The burning encourages the breakdown of starches, called hemicellulose, in the wood into sugars, as well as adding woody, smoky textures to the spirit.

Toasting, effectively, means setting the cask on fire for as long as a distiller demands. Charring requires much less burning, and comes in four integral stages, ranging from 15–55 seconds. Each char levels add a new level of character and flavour to the whisky during maturation.

1. **15 second burn** (ideal for quick-ageing commercial bourbon)
2. **30 second burn** (for sweeter whiskies; adds vanilla, coffee and spicy notes)
3. **35 second burn** (employed for American bourbons and whiskeys; adds earthy, woody spices)
4. **55 second burn** (known as the alligator char, the barrel cracks and peels; adds a lot of smoky flavours, obviously)

Hop-Scotch No.3

There are five regions of Scotland
that produce Scotch.

SPEYSIDE

Half of all Scottish distilleries can
be found in Speyside – the biggest
producer by volume. Elegance and
complexity, refined smokiness; sweeter
tones; fruitiness ranging from ripe
pears to sultanas. The river Spey runs
right through the land, and right
into the distilleries.

Know Your Jack No.1

Have you ever wondered why Jack Daniel's bottles are square, even though the brand itself is too hip to be square? There is a wonderful reason.

In 1895, in Tennessee, whiskey was sold by the barrel, or earthenware jug, not the bottle. If a shop owner wanted to sell it in bottles, he'd fill them himself. It was Jack Daniel's nephew, Lem, who suggested that they should begin bottling their whiskey on the site of the spring, known as Hollow. So the story goes, a local glass salesman – who had "worn out his shoes and his patience going back and forth with samples that a stubborn Jack rejected out of hand" – showed Jack a prototype square bottle, the only bottle he had left. And after thinking it over for a moment, Jack remarked with a smiley, "A square bottle for a square shooter."

Of course, it also helped that the new square bottles prevented the bottles from rolling around when stuck in the back of a horse and carriage, the only mode of transportation back then.

Whisky Wise No.1

Always remember:
Scottish whisky is distilled twice,
Irish whiskey thrice.

The additional distillation creates a
smoother taste and a more subdued
finish as well removing most of the
"congeners" – the esters, tannins,
acetone, aldehydes – the good stuff
that gives whisky distinctive flavour
characteristics and the bad stuff
that gives you a hangover.

Know Your Jack No.2

On the first Friday of every month,
pay day, all employees at Jack Daniel's
get a free bottle of Jack Daniels.
It's guaranteed no one takes
that day off sick.

Johnnie B Goode

Johnnie Walker, who first started
making whisky in 1865, and
perhaps perfected the art with his
Black/Red/Blue Label was, in fact,
a teetotaller.

Whisky At the Movies No.2

In the movie *Superman 3*, after being exposed to Lex Luthor's synthetic kryptonite, Superman goes to a bar, necks a shot and then flicks nuts at superspeed at a mirror, before lasering it with his eyes.

It's the only time in movie history Superman sups a 'ski. Which brand of Scotch is Superman's weapon of choice?

Johnnie Walker Red Label

Most Expensive Whisky

In October 2019, Sotheby's sold at auction the most expensive bottle of whisky ever seen: The Macallan Fine and Rare 60-Year-Old (Cask No.263), distilled in 1926. It sold for $1.9 million.

Doing the maths, a 35ml single shot of this 700ml bottle (20 shots in total) would cost you... $95,000.

Whisky-rific

Calories per 25ml shot of different spirits

Rum	52
Vodka	51
Whisky	55
Tequila	55
Gin	52
Brandy	50
Sambuca	80

Remember: The higher the alcohol content, the higher the calories.

*Add an extra 100 calories if you include a sugary mixer.

Scotch Drink

In 1785, legendary Scottish poet Robert Burns wrote his epic 21-stanza poem celebrating "Scotch Drink":

> *O thou, my muse! guid auld Scotch drink!*
> *Whether thro' wimplin worms thou jink,*
> *Or, richly brown, ream owre the brink,*
> *In glorious faem,*
> *Inspire me, till I lisp an' wink,*
> *To sing thy name!*
> (stanza two)

Burns the bard was particularly romantic about his nation's whisky, and in his tall tale *Tam O'Shanter* (1790) Burns declared his love unconditional:

> *"Inspiring bold John Barleycorn!*
> *What dangers thou canst make us scorn!*
> *Wi' tippeny we fear nae evil;*
> *Wi' usquabae, we'll face the devil!"*

Whisky-a-lingo-go No.2

There are certain terms to use when describing
the characteristics of whisky. Use the words
below to impress your friends.

Light

A term used to describe how *smooth* a whisky
feels on the palate.

Rich

A term used to describe how *strong* a whisky
feels on the palate.

Smoky

A term used to describe how *smoky* a whisky
feels on the palate.

Delicate

A term used to describe how *easy* it is to
identify a whisky's flavours.

You Know You're a Whisky Lover When...

1. Your partner buys you whisky stones and a personalised whisky flask for Christmas.

2. You have ice cube trays specifically used for whisky, and whisky *only*

3. You go on a family holiday to Scotland and only see the inside of a distillery (or three).

Whisky Drinking Games No.1
General Movie

A fun, but gentle, whisky drinking game to play with friends is the General Movie game. Pick a movie and settle in on the sofa with a new bottle of whisky and a tumbler.

When the movie starts you take a sip of whisky every time one of the following items happens. Then, at the end of the movie, see how much whisky you have left. The winner is the person still awake.

Drink every time…
A logo appears / the director's name appears / a character drags on a cigarette / someone swears / the main character's name is said / someone is punched, or kicked / a gun or laser is fired / something explodes / for the duration of a kiss / someone says the word "love" / it rains / the villain appears / the word "you" is said / the main character is in danger

66

You don't know how to drink. Your whole generation, you drink for the wrong reasons. My generation, we drink because it's good, because it feels better than unbuttoning your collar, because we deserve it. We drink, because it's what men do.

99

Roger Sterling,
Mad Men, *season 1, episode 4*

66

I'd much rather be someone's
shot of whiskey than
everyone's cup of tea.

99

Carrie Bradshaw,
Sex and the City

Rye Whiskey

Rye whiskey, predominately adored in the United States and Canada, must have a mash of at least 51 per cent rye and be aged in charred barrels for a minimum of two years. Rye, a type of grass that is a member of the wheat family, has slightly fruity and spicy flavours that are good for cocktails.

The first whiskeys made in the United States were made from rye, but due to corn being the American farmer's bumper crops, there was always plenty left over for whiskey. Rye predates bourbon in that country by more than a century.

Tasting Table: *Wild Turkey, Old Overholt, Jack Daniel's Single Barrel Rye, Rittenhouse, Sazerac, Willetts Distillery*

Hot Scotch

According to the Scotch Whisky
Association (SWA), Scotland's
distilleries saw a whopping 56 per cent
rise in visitors from 2010 to 2018 – a
total number of two million
unique visitors.

Masters of the Dark Arts: American Whiskey

In general, Americans prefer bourbon style whiskeys, but they are partial to the odd Irish and Canadian. Want a good place to start with American whiskeys? These are the world's bestsellers in 2019…

1. Jack Daniel's American Whiskey
2. Crown Royal Canadian Whisky
3. Fireball Canadian Whisky
4. Jim Beam Bourbon Whiskey
5. Jameson Irish Whiskey – 90 per cent of Jameson's is sold outside of Ireland
6. Maker's Mark Bourbon Whiskey
7. Seagram's 7 Crown American Whiskey
8. Evan Williams Bourbon Whiskey
9. Black Velvet Canadian Whisky
10. Johnnie Walker Scotch Whiskey

A Whisky a Day No.1

Despite its high alcohol content, whisky is (in)famous for its restorative qualities.

Don't throw away your medicines away just yet, but here are a few benefits to consider when drinking whisky – in moderation.

1. **LOSE WEIGHT**
    Whisky has no fat and very little sodium. Ingestion of a moderate amount increases energy and, more importantly, decreases the desire for other sugary treats.

2. **HELPS PREVENTS DIABETES**
    Whisky can help regulate the body's insulin and glucose levels, thus assisting in lowering the possibility of contracting typetwo diabetes.

3. **HELPS PREVENT CANCER AND DEMENTIA**
    Ellagic acid is one of the most powerful antioxidant compounds that is also extremely effective in reducing free radicals (a harmful by-product that can open doors to cancer and dementia) – and single malt whisky has high levels of the stuff, thanks to barley.

CHAPTER
THREE

WHISKY-A-GO-GO

Whisky Business No.8

The whisky industry is recognised as the UK's largest single food and drink sector. Incredibly, it accounts for 25 per cent of the UK's entire food and drink exports.

For Scotland, separately, whisky sales drive 80 per cent of all Scottish food and drink exports, and are sold to pretty much every other nation of earth.

Hop-Scotch No.4

LOWLANDS

Only three distilleries are still
in operation in the Lowlands:
Glenkinchie, Bladnoch and
Auchentoshan.

They produce light Scotches,
known as the "Lowland Ladies", that
have malty, zesty flavours with
fruity, citrusy and floral notes.

"

For deafness... take the bile
of a hare with aqua vite and
the milk of a woman's breast
in the same quantity and mix
them well together and put
them in the ear.

"

Whisky, as a cure for deafness, as revealed in
Warren R Dawson's A Leechbook or Collection of
Medical Recipes of the Fifteenth Century.

Whisky Chasers No.3

Whisky chasers always chasin' tail…

Whiskey Sour
Go Get:
Two shots (50ml) of bourbon or rye whiskey
35ml of lemon juice
1 tsp of superfine sugar, or sugar syrup
$\frac{1}{2}$ an egg white
Ice, cracked
Maraschino cherry and/or lemon wedge (garnish)

Make it Right:
Shake the whiskey, juice, sugar and egg white well
    with cracked ice.
Strain into a chilled cocktail glass.
Garnish with a maraschino cherry and/or lemon
    wedge.

Whisky-a-lingo-go No.3

There are a wealth of words used in the whisky industry to describe how the spirit is made. We've distilled the list down to the basics.

ABV

The abbreviation for "alcohol by volume" – the term used to describe the percentage alcohol level in spirits.

Cask Strength

The strength of whisky as it comes from the cask. Whisky cannot be less than 40 per cent ABV. The less a whisky is aged, the higher its ABV will be.

Charring

The process of burning the inside of a cask in order to accentuate the natural compounds in the wood to permeate the spirit once inside the cask.

Chill Filtration

The process of removing any natural substances that turn the whisky cloudy when cold before bottling.

Whisky Playlist No.1

Many an ode has been written 'bout whisky drinkin', but these sure are the best:

1. "Whiskey Bent and Hell Bound", Hank Williams Jr
2. "Poison Whisky", Lynyrd Skynyrd
3. "Whiskey River", Willie Nelson
4. "Whiskey and Wimmen", John Lee Hooker and Canned Heat
5. "It Was the Whiskey Talkin", Jerry Lee Lewis
6. "Moonshine Whiskey", Van Morrison
7. "Whiskey Basin Blues", John Denver
8. "He's Got All the Whiskey", Bo Diddley
9. "Whiskey, Whiskey, Whiskey", John Mayer
10. "The Clouds Are Full of Wine (Not Whiskey or Rye)", Captain Beefheart

Oldest Whisky

As verified by Guinness World Records
in 2018, the oldest bottle of whisky
still left unopened in the world
is Baker's Pure Rye Whiskey, distilled
in 1847.

Whisky-a-lingo-go No.4

SINGLE CASK

A bottle of whisky that has come from
its own individual cask and has not
been mixed with any other whiskies.
Single cask whiskies will bear the cask
information on the bottle, outlining
any specific information in regards to
location the cask was stored, the cask
char and the characteristic/flavours of
the whisky from the cask.

Know Your Whisky

Don't ever say Irish whiskey tastes smoky. Malted barley is dried in closed ovens and is never exposed to smoke.

Scotch, however, *is* defined, effectively, by its smokiness – it's made from barley dried over peat fire. The grain absorbs the smoke.

Act of Union in 1707

When the Act of Union in 1707 brought together England, Wales, and Scotland into the UK, London Parliament commenced taxing Scotch whisky almost immediately. But here's the kicker: they cut the taxes on producing English gin.

Instantly, illegal distilling boomed in Scotland. In Edinburg alone there were apparently around 400 illegal stills making whisky. These illicit whisky makers kept the manufacturing going for master distillers like Bowmore and Glenturret, a few years later. It was not until the Excise Act of 1823 when taxes fell with the reduction of duty by 50 per cent that the majority of whisky making became legal again.

Whisky Wise No.2

Don't bother saving whisky for a rainy day – which is every day in Scotland – because whisky *does not age any further* once it has been bottled.

The only time that time matters to whisky is the time served in the barrel. After that, age is just a number. Unlike wine, whisky can remain in its bottle without changing taste for more than 100 years. But, who waits that long?

Whisky Wisdom No.2

From fermentation to distilling, whisky remains a completely colourless liquid. The "new-make" whisky, as it is known pre-casking, absorbs all of its dark colourings in the cask during the maturation process.

The dark colour comes from the type and age of oak and whatever liquid was formerly contained in the barrel.*

*OK, OK, Spirit Caramel, AKA E150a, can also be added during the maturation phase. This food colouring is a tasteless liquid that many large-scale commercial whisky brands add to their whisky to ensure the liquid has a consistent colour when it is bottled.

Cask A Question No.2

Aside from the American Standard Barrel (ASB), there are a few types of other casks worthy of a mention, in ascending size order:

1. HOGSHEAD (or HOGGIES)
- A hogshead can hold 250 litres, or 335 bottles of 700ml whisky.
- Made from the discarded staves of a bourbon cask but with new oak ends.
- Larger in size than ASBs, they mature whisky intended for longer maturation times.
- Hogheads offer flavour trails of chocolate, orange and dried fruits.

Know Your Oak

Oak is the tree of choice for coopers
(barrel/cask makers) as well as the
whisky industry. Here's why:

1. Oak is strong but can still be
coopered into a cask.

2. It's liquid tight, but porous.

3. It releases vanilla, caramel and nutty
flavours when charred.

4. There are more than 600 varieties
of oak species but only two are used in
cask making: *Quercus alba* (American
oak) and *Quercus robur* (European oak).

Make Your Own Barrel

Beer, wine, dark spirits – no matter what your favourite alcoholic beverage is – you'll know doubt need a barrel. Make your own in these simple steps:

1. Find an American oak tree. Cut it down. Each tree makes three barrels.
2. Air dry the tree for three to six months.
3. Kiln dry the lumber.
4. Cut the tree into pieces the length of your chosen barrel; shave the oak into a trapezoid shape for the staves – 31 staves are needed for each barrel.
5. Steam the staves (to increase wood's flexibility) and bind them into a circular shape using hoops.
6. Toast, or char, the cask. Basically, set it on fire (see page 45)! The higher you burn the barrel the more smoky the flavour; a lower temperature produces fruity-spicy flavours.
7. Once charred, steel hoops are added at the head and belly.
8. Drill a bung hole in the thickest bilge stave. Off you go!

Whisky Wisdom No.3

Inventor, scientist and engineer Nikola
Tesla, best known for designing the
alternating-current (AC) electric system,
and the Tesla Coil, drank whisky every
day. He believed it would help him live
to be 150 years old. He died at the age
of 86 (still very good going).

World Whisky Awards 2020

For the first time ever, in 2020, a Japanese whisky was awarded the highly prestigious prize of world's best single malt whisky. The news shocked the world. Check out these other winners:

Best Blended Whisky – *Dewar's Double 32 Years Old*

Best Blended Malt – *MacNair's Whisky Lum Reek Blended Malt Scotch Whisky, 21 Years Old*

Best Corn Whisky – *Spirit of Haven Distillery Mercurius*

Best Grain Award – *Fuji Single Grain 30 Years Old Small Batch*

Best New Make – *Victoria Caledonian Distillery Peated Mac na Braiche*

Best Rye – *Archie Rose Distilling Co. Rye Malt Whisky*

Best Single Cask Single Malt – *Tamdhu Sandy McIntyre's SC*

Best Single Malt Award – *House of Suntory Hakushu Single Malt 25 Years Old*

Best Canadian Blended Whisky – *J.P. Wiser's Alumni Whisky Series – Darryl Sittler*

Best Flavoured – *Few Spirits Cold Cut Bourbon*

Best Pot Still – *Redbreast Whiskey 21 Years Old*

Best Wheat – *Bainbridge Organic Distillers Two Islands Hokkaido Cask*

Best Bourbon – *Ironroot Republic Distillery Harbinger*

Best Tennessee – *Uncle Nearest Premium Whiskey 1820 Single Barrel*

Best Single Barrel Bourbon – *Rebel Yell Bourbon Single Barrel 10 Years Old*

Best Whisky Design – *Jura Whisky 21 Years Old – Tide*

Know Your Jack No.3

1. Legend has it that Jack became so frustrated with his safe that he kicked it and shattered his left big toe. He got gangrene and the toe was surgically removed, followed by his foot, then his leg. He died six years later from complications from the original infection.

2. Jack Daniel's, in Lynchburg, Tennessee, is built on the site of Cave Spring Hollow, a sediment-free spring with a steady temperature of 13.3 degrees Celsius (56 degrees Fahrenheit). It is the whiskey's singular greatest natural resource. The cave's limestone layers strip all the iron completely from the water. Every single bottle of Jack is made with water from this spring.

3. Jack Daniel's is the only distiller in the world that makes barrels for its own product.

4. Approximately 2,500 barrels of whiskey are made each day.

5. Jack Daniel's recipe = 80 per cent corn, 12 per cent barley and 8 per cent rye. During the distillation process, these grains are mixed with yeast and mash from a previous batch, and iron-free water from Cave Spring Hollow. This ferments for six days before being single-distilled in copper.

6. Jack Daniel's original and most famous whiskey is called "Old No. 7", but no one truly knows the number's significance. Lucky number seven?

7. Tennessee's Moore County, where the Jack Daniel's distillery is located, has been a dry county since Prohibition, so you have to go to the next state to buy a bottle.

Whisky Wisdom No.4

July 27
International Scotch Whisky Day.

See you there.

Whisky Wise No.3

Of the flavour in the whisky,
60–80 per cent originates from the
cask it was matured in.

Moonshine

Hilts (Steve McQueen),
tasting moonshine: "Wow!"

Hendley (James Garner),
tasting moonshine: "Wow!"

Goff (Jud Taylor),
tasting moonshine: "Wow!"

The Great Escape, *1963*

Moonshine is the rather brilliant name given to un-aged
whisky, made from fermented potatoes, where the alcohol
content is usually as high as the moon is far! Moonshine received
its name from the fact that it was made illegally under the light
of the moon following the merger of England and Scotland
under the "Acts of Union" and dramatic rise of the taxes
(especially after English Malt Tax of 1725) almost killed
the burgeoning whisky business.

Whisky-lingo-a-go-go No.5

'Nosing'

Before you even dare take your first
sip of whisky, stick your nose in your
whisky glass and take a deep inhalation
of the aromas swirling around the
glass. This is called nosing.

The Copper Dog

Way back when, when the world of whisky was just starting to become industrialised, dishonest distillery workers would often try to smuggle whisky home with them. So desperate were they for a dram, they devised a device known as the "copper dog", a long copper pipe with a coin soldered on one end and a cork on the other. The dog was dipped into a cask and filled with whisky… and then concealed down the trouser leg of the employee as they coolly walked out front door. Albeit with an awkward limp.

Whisky Wisdom No.5

If you're drinking to forget,
don't hit the whisky.

A study published in 2010 by the
US National Institutes of Health
recommended that adults who
consumed "one to six portions a week"
of whisky were 50 per cent less likely
to suffer dementia as non-drinkers
and heavy drinkers.

A whisky a day keeps the
doctors at bay.

Hop-Scotch No.5

ISLAY
(pronounced "eye-luh")

With eight distilleries, Islay is the
big boy of whisky-producing islands;
Islay is 25 miles long. The island is
covered in peat and doused in sea
spray. Smoky, salty, peaty notes.

"

The light music of whiskey
falling into a glass – an
agreeable interlude.

"

James Joyce

CHAPTER
FOUR

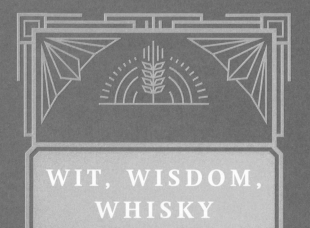

WIT, WISDOM, WHISKY

66

Being moderately taken, whisky slows the age, cuts phlegm, helps digestion, cures the dropsy, it heals the strangulation, keeps and preserves the head from whirling, the tongue from lisping, the stomach from wombling, the guts from rumbling, the hands from shivering, the bones from aching... and truly it is a sovereign liquor if it be orderly taken.

99

Raphaël Holinshed,
The Chronicles of England, Scotland and Ireland, 1577

A Whisky a Day No.2

What's that? Even more health benefits to whisky?
Yes.

4. HELPS LOWER STROKE RISKS
A sip or three of whisky will thin out your
blood, which will, in turn, lower the chance of
blood clots and strokes.

5. STRESS RELIEF
Whisky is stuffed full of alcohol – an active
ingredient much loved for lowering stress and
tension when required.

6. AIDS DIGESTION
Whisky is the best digestif at the end of a large
meal. Whisky's high alcohol content stimulates
pepsin, an enzyme in the stomach that breaks
down the proteins that you've ingested, and
helps push them through the digestive system.

"

My God, so much I like to
drink Scotch that
sometimes I think my name
is Igor Stra-whiskey.

"

Igor Stravinsky

66

Never delay kissing
a pretty girl or opening a
bottle of whiskey.

99

Ernest Hemingway

66

When life hands you lemons,
make Whiskey Sours.

99

W C Fields

❝

My family was a bunch of
drunks. When I was six
I came up missing, they put
my picture on a bottle
of Scotch.

❞

Rodney Dangerfield

"

It is true that whisky
improves with age. The older
I get, the more I like it.

"

Robert Black

66

The true pioneer of
civilization is not the
newspaper, not religion, not
the railroad but whiskey!

99

Mark Twain

"

What whiskey will not cure,
there is no cure for.

"

Irish Proverb

66

While I can't walk on water,
I can certainly wobble on
whisky.

99

Ashwin Sanghi

Hop-Scotch No.6

CAMPBELTOWN

A small coastal town at the tip of Kintyre, now has just three distilleries (reduced from 30). Salty and peaty notes – influences from the sea.

Whisky Drinking Games No.2
Confidence Man

What you need:
A bottle of whisky (not the good stuff)
A tumbler
A coin
Four friends

The Rules
With your group of friends, decide how much
whisky you are willing to be confident about
drinking in one go – following the flip of coin.
Fill your tumbler, decide heads or tails and flip
the coin. If you chose correctly, don't drink. Feel
good. If you chose poorly, drink.

Whisky Chasers No.4

Whisky chasers always chasin' tail...

Whiskey Smash
Go Get
Two shots (50ml) of bourbon or rye whiskey
$^1/_2$ lime, cut into wedges, one reserved as a garnish
2 cucumber slices
5 sprigs of fresh mint, keeping the best back for
   the garnish
100ml cold lemonade
Ice cubes

Make it Right
- Muddle the lime, cucumber and mint at the bottom of a tumbler.
- Fill the glass with ice cubes.
- Pour in the whisky.
- Top up with lemonade.
- Garnish with mint, a lime wedge.

Make Your Mark

The world's oldest operating
bourbon whiskey distillery is Maker's
Mark in Loretto, Kentucky.
This distillery has been distilling
bourbon since 1805.

It is now recognised as a National
Historic Landmark.

Hot Toddy

Feeling poorly? Here's your medicine:

Go Get:
50ml whisky (of your choice)
3 tsp honey
$\frac{1}{2}$ cinnamon stick
$\frac{1}{2}$ lemon, juiced and sliced
2 cloves
200ml boiling water

Make it Right:
- Whisk the whisky and honey together. Pour into your mug.
- Add the $\frac{1}{2}$ cinnamon stick to your mug, then top up with 200ml boiling water.
- Add a splash of lemon juice and a lemon wheel (studded with the cloves).
- Feel better immediately.

Holy Water

In April 2020, Pope Francis, the leader of the Catholic Church around the world, was handed a bottle of Oban Malt Whisky during a visit to a Rome's Scots College priest school.

When handed the bottle, the Pope declared "Questa e la vera acqua santa," which when translated means "This is the real holy water".

The moment was caught on video camera. The Vatican's media office has since censored the footage.

As seen on thedrinksbusiness.com, 20 April 2020
by Edith Hancock

Whisky Wise No.4

Whisky has more than 100 complex flavour components, more than double that of cognac and rum, it's nearest nemeses. Vodka has ten-ish.

Jog on, voddie!

Whisky Wise No.5

Did you know that the hourglass-
shaped device bartenders around
the world use to measure and pour a
correct unit of whisky is called a jigger.

In the United States, a jigger is 1.5 oz
for a shot. A "pony shot" usually
means 1 oz.

In Scotland and Ireland, the two shot
sizes are 35ml, a single, and 70ml.

In England and Wales, the two shot
sizes are 25ml, a single, and 70ml.

Cask A Question No.3

And other, less common, types of barrels used in the whisky maturation process:

2. BARRIQUE
- Larger than ASB; Holds 250–300 litres.
- Made from French oak and American white oak.
- Used predominately in the wine industry and to mature single malts.

3. BUTT
- Holds 475–500 litres, or 450 bottles of whisky.
- Butts mature whisky over a period greater than 20 years.
- Traditionally made from Spanish oak.

4. PUNCHEON
- 500 litres, or 450 bottles of whisky.
- Typically made with Spanish oak staves.

5. PORT PIPE
- 550–650 litres, or 550 bottles of whisky.
- First employed to mature port wine.
- Port pipes are then used in the final years of maturation for Scotch whisky.
- Adds clove, nutmeg and strawberry and raspberry flavours to the whisky.

6. MADEIRA DRUM
- 600–650 litres, or 600 bottles of whisky.
- Used in the final years of whisky maturation.

Barrels used in the production of rum, wine, cognac, madeira, marsala and even beer, are also used.

Whisky Wise No.6

There are twenty
35ml shots
to a 700ml bottle of whisky
(UK size).

Whisky Business No.9

The world has been catching up to whisky
production in the last few decades but,
currently, the top five largest regional
producers are:

1. SCOTCH WHISKY
(1.3 billion bottles sold in 2019)

2. IRISH WHISKEY
(135 million bottles sold in 2019)

3. BOURBON
(Kentucky-based, or otherwise)

4. CANADIAN WHISKY

5. TENNESSEE WHISKEY
(Jack Daniels sold 150 million bottles in 2019!)

Know Your Jack No.4

Jack Daniels is the United States No.1 whiskey brand and, probably, the most famous whiskey brand on the planet. But how much do you know about this legendary whisky maker?

1. Jack learned how to make whiskey at the age of 6.
2. Jack Daniel's is the oldest registered distillery in America.
3. Jack's birth records were destroyed in a fire; his precise birthdate is unknown. But "September 1850" is inscribed on his tombstone.
4. Jack Daniel was diminutive: just 5 feet 2 inches tall and wore a size four shoe.
5. It was then-enslaved Nathan "Nearest" Green that taught Jack how to make whiskey. After emancipation, Jack made Nearest Green the brand's first-ever master distiller; the two families continue to work together.

Masters of the Dark Arts: Canadian Whisky

Corn and rye whiskey makers in Canada are hot on the heels, these days, of Irish whiskey and Scotch. While Crown Royal is the undisputed king of Canadian whisky, in terms of heritage and sales, these are other brands are making quite the name for themselves too. Who will you pick up first?

1. Crown Royal
2. Forty Creek
3. Gibson's
4. Wiser's
5. Pendleton Whisky
6. Canadian Club
7. Black Velvet
8. Seagram
9. Caribou Crossing
10. Kirkland Canadian Whisky

Saint Patrick

It was Saint Patrick who brought distillation to Ireland in 432 AD. What a saint.

Celebrate his day on the 17th March every year.

All he asks in return is to know these fine Irish whiskeys well by then, my friend:

Winners of the Irish Whiskey Awards 2019

Best Irish Single Pot Still – *Middleton Barry Crockett Legacy*

Best Irish Single Malt (12 years and younger) – *Dunville's PX Cask 12 Year Old*

Best Irish Single Malt (13 years and older) –
Teeling Brabazon Volume 1

Best Irish Blended Whiskey (RRP of less than €60) –
Jameson Black Barrel

Best Irish Blended Whiskey (RRP of more than €60)
– *Jameson 18 Year Old Bow Street*

Best Irish Single Cask – *The Irishman 17 Year Old*

Best Irish Cask Strength – *Redbreast 12 Year Old Cask Strength*

Best Irish Single Grain – *Method & Madness Single Grain Virgin Spanish Oak Finish*

Best New Irish Whiskey – *Kilbeggan Small Batch Rye*

Best Irish Whiskey Overall – *The Irishman 17 Year Old*

Whiskey By the Numbers No.2

Bourbon is a whiskey made up of at least 51 per cent corn.

Rye whiskey must have at least 51 per cent rye.

Wheat whiskey must have 51 per cent of wheat.

A corn whiskey must have at least 80 per cent corn.

66

There is no bad whiskey.
There are only some
whiskeys that aren't as good
as others.

99

Raymond Chandler
Chandler drank nothing but bourbon for
eight days straight as he completed his masterpiece,
The Blue Dahlia.

CHAPTER
FIVE

MESSAGE IN
A BOTTLE

Whisky Chasers No.5

Whisky chasers always chasin' tail…

Highball

Go Get:
Two shots (50ml) whisky
Soda water or sparkling water
Wheel or slice of lemon

Make it Right:
Fill a tall tumbler with ice.
Drown the ice with the whisky and stir with a
    spoon to cool it all down.
Top up with soda or sparking water. Give it another
    good stir.
Garnish with lemon wheel or slice.

How to Drink Whisky

For many, yourself included hopefully, whisky
is not a spirit you guzzle or neck in one. Whisky
demands your appreciation… and your time. Drink
it as it desires, and your patience will be rewarded.

1. Gaze at the whisky in the glass. Notice the
    shade of caramel. Let your eyes start the feast.

2. Nose the whisky. A strong inhalation; let the
    whisky soak into your lungs.

3. Smell again (the first sniff will be all alcohol;
    the second and third sniff will be full of
    pungent aromatics).

4. Take a sip. Don't swallow. Hold the spirit in
    your mouth.

5. Roll the whisky over your tongue. Chew on it.
    Let the flavours build.

6. Swallow. And breath a deep breath out.

Whisky-a-lingo-go No.6

There are a wealth of words used in the whisky industry to describe how the spirit is made. We've distilled the list down to the basics.

PEAT
A layer of earth that lays below the topsoil. Peat is made up of grasses, plants, tree roots and mosses that have been compressed for millennia. When dried it can be employed as a fuel. The peat burns with a very consistent, high temperature with a thick acrid blue smoke. When peat is burnt, dry malted barley grain absorbs the peaty flavour, which then gets carried through the rest of the whisky making process.

GRIST
Malted barley that has been milled (ground up)
into a powder, so that it can be added to water to
become mash. The natural sugars present in the
barley will dissolve.

POT STILL
Copper pot stills have excellent conductive
qualities. Alcoholic wash is heated at the base,
alcohol vapours rises up the neck and then
condensed again back into a liquid spirit.

Whisky Wise No.7

spiritus frumenti

Latin,
for "the spirit of grain".

Whisky Wise No.8

In 1830, at the height of American's
importation, and love affair, of whiskey
from Ireland and Scotch, America's
consumption of alcohol, per capita, is
enough to give you a hangover.

It peaked at approximately 1.7 bottles
of whiskey, *per person, per week*. That's
88 bottles a year. *Each*.

Prohibition, thankfully, began in 1920.

Whisky Business No.10

Kentucky is home to more barrels of maturing bourbon than people. In 2019, Kentucky's population was approx. 4.5 million people. Barrels of whiskey = 9.1 million.

Whisky Business No.11

Most whisky distilleries around the
world send and keep casks of whisky
produced by other distilleries, their
competitors, in their warehouses for
maturation. Why? For the collective
safety of all the whisky.

Whisky is a highly flammable liquid
– so if one distillery goes up in smoke
(great for flavour), they
wouldn't lose their entire stock.

Know Your Glass

While the classic whisky tumbler is the most common of all whisky glasses, there are a few other types of glasses, each one designed for its own singular purpose.

1. TUMBLER

Also known as a "rocks glass", the "old fashioned glass" and "lowball', the tumbler, with its wide and robust base, is perfect for your weekday whisky wind downs. But it isn't very good for nosing.

2. TULIP

Also known as a "copita-style" glass, or the "dock" glass, the tulip is based on the traditional Spanish glass used to sample sherry. Master distillers use a tulip glass as it is perfect for nosing wines. It was once named the "dock" glass due to its long stem, which prevented the drinker's hand from getting too close to the nose; its bowl shape and narrow rim helps concentrate aromas.

3. GLENCAIRN
Perfect for giving whisky a good swirl, a good technique to open up the aromas.

4. HIGHBALL
A Highball is a tall tumbler, basically, and ideal for whisky cocktails and Scotch and soda. A highball allows for plenty of ice, spirit and mixer. Sure, you could use a pint glass – but that's not classy, is it?

5. SNIFTER
Also known as a "balloon" and "brandy bowl", a snifter is perfectly shaped for swilling and swirling.

6. THE SHOT
You know the one. For heathens, mostly. Bless 'em.

Whisky at the Movies No.3

The actor Humphrey Bogart, the greatest male star of classic American cinema, and star of *Casablanca* and *The Maltese Falcon*, was a big whisky chaser, and, according to legend, said these last unscripted words on his deathbed. "I should never have switched from Scotch to martinis."

Whisky Business No.12

Of course, it isn't just Scotland, Ireland, Canada, Japan and the United States that make whisky; other nations have begun to get in on the act. Keep an eye on these guys:

GERMANY
- German-made whisky started 30 years ago.
- German whiskies are of various styles such as single malts, blends, and bourbon.
- There are in total 23 distilleries in Germany producing whisky.

TAIWAN
- Taiwan has only one whiskey distillery – Kavalan.
- The distillery produces nine million bottles (750,000 cases) a year.

FINLAND
- There are currently four operational distilleries in Finland.

AUSTRALIA
- Australia currently has 26 whisky distilleries; Tasmania is the hotspot.

Masters of the Dark Arts: Scotch Whisky

A nonsense list, we admit, as there are so many makers of lovely Scotch, but for you beginners out there, these Scotch makers are the masters:

1. **Lagavulin (Islay)**
   Founded in: 1816

2. **Laphroaig (Islay)**
   Founded in: 1815

3. **The Macallan (Speyside)**
   Founded in: 1824

4. **Johnnie Walker (Ayrshire)**
   Founded in: 1820

5. Talisker (Skye)
Founded in: 1830
Best-known expression: 10 Year

6. Ardbeg (Islay)
Founded in: 1815

7. Glenfiddich (Speyside)
Founded in: 1886

8. Glenmorangie (Highland)
Founded in: 1843

9. Bowmore (Islay)
Founded in: 1779

10. The Glenlivet (Speyside)
Founded in: 1824

Water Water Everywhere...

Water is key to the whisky's flavour and overall character. Distilleries tend to stay close to a water source, especially if there is access to pure, fresh, and iron-free water. Lochs in Scotland, for example, and nature spring wells and rivers in the United States.

On the Isle of Islay, in Scotland, the nearby water flows over peaty soil that contains decayed seaweed and sphagnum (a type of moss) that release phenols. It is these phenols that are the compounds responsible for the smoky taste of really good Scotch.

Bourbon or Tennessee Whiskey?

What's the difference between Bourbon
and Tennessee whiskey? It's a long-ask
question and one with a simple answer:
the Lincoln County Process.

Bourbon and Tennessee whiskeys are both
made with at least 51 per cent corn and aged in
charred new oak barrels. Prior to the whiskey
designated as Tennessee is placed inside its
cask for maturation, Tennessee whiskey is
filtered through about 3 metres (10 feet) of
tightly packed vats of homemade sugar-maple
charcoal for 10 to 12 days, a process known
as the Lincoln County Process. This filtration
yields a smoother whiskey. That's it!

Case in Point

In the United States, a case of whiskey usually means the equivalent of 12 quarts. A quart is a quarter of a gallon, or 2 US pints*.

Everywhere else in the world, a case of whiskey means 12 bottles of almost any capacity between 1 pint and 2 pints*. There are roughly 1.5 pints to every bottle of whisky.

*US pints and UK imperial pints are not the same volume. A US pint = 475 ml; a UK pint = 568 ml.

66

There's a special rung in
hell reserved for people who
waste good Scotch.

99

Lt. Archie
Inglourious Basterds, *2009*

Whisky Business No.13

A huge expense of making bourbon is the industry-standard American Standard barrel (ASB), which costs approximately $250 per barrel. Approximately 2,500 barrels of whiskey are made each day at Jack Daniels. Barrelling occurs only in May, after maturation.

Whisky History No.2
The Whiskey Rebellion of 1794

Whiskey wended its merry way to the new American colonies in the 1600s when Irish, English and Scottish immigrants searched for a new frontier. For a time, whisky was currency, allowing settlers to trade and build businesses.

A few years after the United States was born, in 1776, young distillers and farmers of Scottish and Irish descent were imposed with a heavy tax handed down to them by then Secretary of Treasury, Alexander Hamilton, in 1791. There was an uprising that escalated into the Whiskey Rebellion of 1794, which for first US President George Washington was the first ever challenge to the newly formed federal authority. Hamilton's tax was repealed in 1802. For the next century, whisky making and whisky drinking exploded.

Corn Whiskey

Once the tipple of choice for America's poorest peoples, and the original moonshine, corn whiskey is now again enjoying a full-scale renaissance and is, indeed, the people's whiskey – Jack Daniels, the world's largest whiskey brand, is a corn whiskey.

All corn whiskey's must be made from a minimum of 80 per cent corn mash, but there is no minimum cask ageing time and the casks do not need to be charred in oak barrels, though two years is the standard.

Tasting Table: *Bowen's, Georgia Moon, Balcones, Bowsaw, Heaven Hill*

66

For relaxing times,
make it Suntory time.

99

Bill Murray's Bob,
Lost in Translation, *2003*

.

Whisky Drinking Games No.3
Who Me?

What you need:
A bottle of whisky (not the good stuff)
A tumbler
A group of friends

The Rules
- A person in the group has to ask their group of friends a "Who's most likely…" question. Everyone has to then point to the person they believe fits the bill. For example: "Who's most likely to… get sunburn on holiday?" Whoever gets pointed at must answer, "Who me?"
- The number of fingers that are pointed at that person equals the number of fingers that person must drink.

World Whisky Calender

World Whisky Day – every third
Saturday in May each year.

Whisky History No.3

In the 1860s, whisky drinking was still second to wine, the overwhelmingly tipple of choice for the drinking classes.

However, in 1858, phylloxera, a plague of louse, travelled from the US (presumably by boat) and destroyed the European continent's vineyards for a period of 15 years. Nine-tenths of the grape crops were lost with a sustained devastation of up to 40 per cent of all wine crops, a cost of more than 10 billion francs. It became known as the Great French Wine Blight.

With a scarcity of wine (and brandy) across all of Europe during this time, wine lovers turned to whisky and, from this point on, the whisky industry saw a surge in popularity it has never lost. It was during this time that wine barrels – going unused – were used to mature Scotch whisky, a practise that is still popular today.

CHAPTER
SIX

WHISKY
CHASER

Know Your Cask

Remember:
The smaller the cask, the faster the maturation of the whisky.

Remember:
Up to 60–80 % of the flavour of the final whisky is thought to be gleaned from the cask it matures in.

Remember:
Casks can be used up to four times when making Scotch. After this, the cask ceases to add flavour.

Whisky Wise No.9

A bottle of 750ml whisky is equivalent
to 17 bottles of 5 per cent ABV beer.*

A sobering thought.

* General rule of thumb is that a shot is equivalent to a bottle –
not pint – of beer.

Whisky Business No.14

Have you ever compared the size of your
US and UK whisky bottles and wondered why
there is a slight difference in size? It's because
there are actually two sizes of whisky bottles,
and the difference is all down to where the
whisky was produced.

A European spirit bottle is 23.7 Fl oz (700ml).
This is the standard spirit bottle size currently
used by countries in the European Union. It is
known as a European metric "quart", and
is not used in the United States.

In the United States, a "fifth" is used instead.
Measuring 25.4 U.S. Fl oz (750ml) – a US metric
"quart". This is the most common spirit bottle
size in the United States. Americans get more
bang for their buck than the Brits.

Make Your Mark

As you know by now, when it comes to whisky, the United States and Ireland spell the word with an "e," while Scotland, Japan, Canada and everywhere else, spells it without: "whisky".

However, there is one exception to this famous rule.

And it's called Maker's Mark.

Maker's Mark – the brand with the signature red wax cork – chooses the Scottish way to spell whisky, even though it's a Kentucky-based bourbon. Why? To pay homage to their Scottish roots, of course.

Make your mark, indeed.

Whisky Wisdom No.6

An opened bottle of whisky can
remain good in its original bottle, or
decanted, for five years.

Any longer… and I'll come pick it up.
Shame on you.

Whisky Business No.15

In 2019, 1.3 billion bottles of
Scotch whisky were sold.

If you laid all those bottles
cork-to-base vertically, they
would stretch 350,000 kilometres
(217,000 miles), or 90 per cent
of the distance to the moon!

Moonshine, indeed.

Whisky Business No.16

Like gin before it, whisky – and whiskey – is currently have a renaissance in the home-buying consumer market, as well as the home-made craft market.

Worldwide sales of Irish whiskey have risen by more than 300 per cent in the last ten years. Today, more than 200 bottles of Irish whiskey are sold every minute. Jameson's remains the world's preferred Irish whiskey brand. Can you make a better one?

Whisky Business No.17

Glenfiddich remains the world's best-selling single malt whisky. It represents 35 per cent of all Scotch whisky single malt sales.

The other nine world bestselling single malts are from Glenlivet, Macallan, Singleton, Glenmorangie, Balvenie, Monkey Shoulder, Laphoraig, Aberlour and Glen Grant.

66

Love makes the world go
round? Not at all.
Whiskey makes it go round
twice as fast.

99

Compton MacKenzie

66

When you work hard all day with your head and know you must work again the next day what else can change your ideas and make them run on a different plane like whiskey?

99

Ernest Hemingway

Masters of the Dark Arts: Japanese Whisky

Not sure where to start with Japanese whisky? Get nosing. With more than 20 distilleries and counting, Japanese whiskey has gone global.

Here's some to get you started for ten (they were among the world's most well reviewed in 2019).

1. House of Suntory Whisky Toki
2. Nikka Whiskey from the Barrel
3. Yamazaki Distillery Reserve Single Malt Whisky
4. Hibiki Japanese Harmony Suntory Whisky
5. Chichibu Ichiro's Malt & Grain Japanese Blended Whisky
6. Ichiro's Malt & Grain Chichibu Blended Whisky
7. Hakushu 12 Year Old
8. Taketsuru Pure Malt
9. Yamazakura 963
10. Yamazaki 12 Year Old

What's in a Whisky: Barley

Barley is a cereal grain and belongs in the family of grasses. When its seed is not distilled into single malt Scotch whisky, barley can be found in breakfast cereals and flour.

It was King Edward I whom, at the beginning of the 14th century, introduced his new-fangled measurement system – based on barley.

Three barleycorns equal one inch.
Thirty-nine (39) barleycorns equal one foot.

One hundred and seventeen (117) barleycorns equal one yard.

If you have a size nine foot (40 in the EU), your foot is the length of 29 barleycorns.

What's In A Whiskey: Corn

Corn, or maize as it is also known, is a cereal grain that is also part of the grass family. After sugar cane, corn is the most grown crop in the world. For a corn whiskey, such as Jack Daniels, the legal requirement of corn is no less than 80 per cent – that's fine, in the United States, there are more than 69 million football field-sized fields dedicated to growing corn.

An ear, or cob of corn, is part of the flower and an individual kernel is a seed, and these are only distilled when the corn and the kernels are dry and the stalks are brown are dry. The most common corn used in whiskey is yellow dent field corn No.1.

While you're here: did you know that an average ear of corn has 800 kernels in 16 rows?

What's In A Whiskey: Rye

Rye is a grass, a member of the wheat
family (and closely related to barley)
and grown predominately in the world
as a grain. Today, rye grain is used for
the production of flour, bread, beer, rye
vodka and rye whiskey!

66

Happiness is having a
rare steak, a bottle of whisky
and a dog to
eat the rare steak.

99

Johnny Carson

66

The water was not fit to
drink. To make it palatable,
we had to add whisky.
By diligent effort, I learnt
to like it.

99

Winston Churchill

What's In A Whisky: Wheat

Like rye, barley and corn, wheat is a member of the grass family. Its seed is cultivated as a cereal grain, which when milled can be used for bread, flour and, when distilled, for whisky!

Approximately 95 per cent of the wheat the people of earth consume is called common wheat (*Triticum aestivum*).

World trade in wheat is greater than for all other crops combined.

"

Too much of anything is bad,
but too much good whiskey
is barely enough.

"

Mark Twain

Friar John Cor

The stereotype of the drunk monk from such medieval legends as Robin Hood stem from the reality that monks really did progress the evolution of alcoholic beverages, including champagne (famously Dom Perignon: "I am drinking stars!"), beer and whisky.

Friar John Cor, a Scottish monk, and a servant at the court of King James IV, was perhaps the archetype on which all drunk monks are based. It was Cor who is responsible for the first known written reference to Scotch Whisky, June 1, 1495. The king commanded he make whisky, and he did.

"To Brother John Cor, by order of the King, to make *aqua vitae* VIII bolls of malt."
Exchequer Rolls 1494–95, Vol x, p. 487

66

I like my whisky old
and my women young.

99

Errol Flynn

Frisky Whisky

Don Draper, the whisky-soaked Manhattan
advertising executive
from *Mad Men*, loved a blended
whisky called Canadian Club. Draper also
knew how to order a whisky at a bar.
These are his killer lines:

"Big and Brown."

"Simple…but significant."

66

I have never in my life
seen a Kentuckian who didn't
have a gun, a pack of cards
and a jug of whiskey.

99

Andrew Jackson

66

I wish to live to 150 years old,
but the day I die, I wish it
to be with a cigarette in one
hand and a glass of whiskey
in the other.

99

Ava Gardner

66

Whisky is liquid sunshine.

99

George Bernard Shaw

Whisky Chasers

Princess Margaret
Famous Grouse, with a splash of water

Queen Elizabeth II's sister was a famous drinker and smoker, so much so that famous chef Gordon Ramsey once said of her: "She started with Scotch and went on drinking for three hours. The ashtray had to be changed every three minutes. I find it hard to believe that she could have tasted the pudding."

Anthony Burgess
Scotch

The author of the masterpiece A Clockwork Orange, a novel the Rolling Stones manager Andrew Loog Oldham (a friend of Burgess') revealed was written "in a writing frenzy, buoyed by Scotch, amphetamine and no sleep."

"
Always carry a flagon of
whiskey in case of snakebite
and furthermore always carry
a small snake.

"

W C Fields

66

I always take Scotch whisky
at night as a preventive
of toothache. I have never
had the toothache; and what
is more, I never intend
to have it.

99

Mark Twain

Whisky Drinking Games No.4
Drunkopoly

What you need:
Whisky (not the good stuff)
Shot glasses
A group of friends
Monopoly

The Rules
Play Monopoly as you normally do. However, add a sip of whisky into the mix every time money changes hands, profit or loss.

Whisky Chasers No.6

Whisky chasers always chasin' tail…

Irish Coffee

Go Get:
50ml cold double cream
2 tbsp soft brown muscovado sugar
50ml Irish whiskey – has to be Irish!
200ml freshly brewed coffee
Nutmeg, to top

Make it Right:
- Fill your chosen glass or mug with hot water and leave to stand.
- Make a pot of fresh coffee.

- Whip the double cream until bubbles disappear and it begins to thicken; put into the fridge.
- Dissolve the sugar in 2 tablespoons of hot water in a small pan and bring to the boil. Let it go nice and syrupy.
- Take the sugar off the heat and stir in the Irish whiskey.
- Empty the glass of hot water and pour the whiskey mixture in, then stir in the freshly made coffee.
- Take the cream out of the fridge, whisk it once.
- Pour the cream over the back of a spoon onto the coffee/whiskey.
- Grate nutmeg over the top.

The Five Flavours of Whisky

Whisky is renowned for having more than 100 flavour profiles, but these can be distilled into five simple headline categories.

FRAGRANT AND FLORAL
Flavours of fresh cut flowers and grass, green and citrus fruit. These are commonly light and delicate whiskies.

MALTY AND DRY
Flavours of dustiness and nuttiness, flour or cereal grains; sweet oak.

FRUITY AND SPICY
Flavours of ripe fruit; spices (cinnamon and nutmeg).

RICH AND ROUND
Flavours of dried fruits – figs, dates, sultanas. These whiskies have depth to their flavour.

SMOKY AND PEATY
Smoke makes a great Scotch. Peaty, charred wood flavours.

66

I'm a simple man. All I
want is enough sleep for
two normal men, enough
whiskey for three, and
enough women for four.

99

Joel Rosenberg

185

Whisky Mixers

If you're not man enough to enjoy your whisky with nothing more than a few drops of water, then, sure, why not pour some of these wussy mixers on your whisky.

GINGER ALE
The perfect sidekick for whisky. Ginger ale has a long list of complex flavour ranges, from sweet and hot to medicinal and earthy. Even a fresh ginger chunk will work magic in the glass.

SWEET VERMOUTH
The vanilla, orange and clove flavours from sweet vermouth all pair well with whisky.

SODA WATER
Cool your whisky down with some chilled bubbles.
Be sure to add a squeeze of lemon or better yet,
fill the glass with lemonade ice cubes. Whisky and
soda – Margaret Thatcher's favourite tipple.

COCA-COLA
Jack and Coke – the most ordered drink at any bar.
The crisp bitter sweetness of Coca-Cola pair well
with any bourbon-style whiskey. A squeeze of lime
will temper the sugar buzz of the Coke.

LEMON
Lemon juice can neutralise a whisky's in-your-face
booziness. Any citrus oils or fruit in your glass
swirled with whisky will taste almost… curative!

"

Fifty year old Macallan – a
particular favourite of yours,
I understand.

"

Javier Bardem's Silva to James Bond,
Skyfall, 2012

66

So here's what, you slip me
a bottle of bourbon, a little
glass and some ice.

99

Jack Torrance,
The Shining, *1980. Though Jack asked for a
bourbon, he is actually slipped a bottle of Jack Daniels –
a Tennessee whiskey.*

Whisky Glossary

There are a wealth of words used in the whisky industry to describe how the spirit is made. We've distilled the list down to the basics.

COLUMN STILL
A large industrial still that allows for continuous and automated distillation of commercial grain whiskies.

CONDENSATION
A part of the distillation process where alcohol vapours turn into a liquid spirit, via cooling apparatus that form part of the still.

COOPER
The persons responsible for making barrels and casks for whisky maturation. The process itself is called coopering.

DISTILLATION
The process of transforming alcoholic wash into highly alcoholic liquid spirit by heating the wash, allowing alcohol vapours to evaporate and rise up the neck of the still where they are condensed to form a liquid again.

DRAFF
The leftovers from the mashing process – barley husks and other remains of the grain. These are collected, dried and compressed in to pellets and sold as animal feed.

Whisky Playlist No.2

Get your dram on while you listen to these popular odes to whisky…

1. 'Whiskey on the Rocks' – AC/DC
2. 'Take Your Whiskey Home' – Van Halen
3. 'Whiskey in the Jar' – Thin Lizzy
4. 'Alabama Song (Whiskey Bar)' – The Doors
5. 'Whiskey 'n' Mama' – ZZ Top
6. 'Lace and Whiskey' – Alice Cooper
7. 'Whiskey Rock-A-Roller' – Lynyrd Skynyrd
8. 'Deacon Blues' – Steely Dan
9. 'One Bourbon, One Scotch, One Beer' – George Thorogood
10. 'Whiskey Man' – The Who
11. 'Streams of Whiskey' – The Pogues